ASCENDING

Other works by Richard A. Long

Black Americana (1985)

The Black Tradition in American Dance (1989)

African Americans: A Portrait (1993)

Grown Deep: Essays on the Harlem Renaissance (1998)

One More Time: Harlem Renaissance History and Historicism (2007)

Maya Angelou: A Glorious Celebration (Co-authored with Marcia Ann
        Gillespie and Rosa Johnson Butler, 2008)

Afro-American Writing: An Anthology of Prose and Poetry
        (Edited with Eugenia W. Collier, 1990)

Black Writers and the American Civil War (1989)

Negritude: Essays and Studies (Edited with Albert H. Berrian, 1967)

ASCENDING
AND OTHER POEMS

by
Richard A. Long

Third World Press
Chicago, Illinois

Third World Press Commemorative Edition
Originally a publication of the DuSable Museum of African American History, Inc.
Printed in the United States of America

Photos of Richard Long by Susan Ross

ISBN 13: 978-0-88378-350-4

CONTENTS

PUBLISHER'S ACKNOWLEDGMENT, PREROGATIVE AND APPRECIATION

In my short tenure on this earth, I have been privileged to have had intimate, long involvements with a significant number of brilliant people: Gwendolyn Brooks, Amiri Baraka, Barbara Ann Sizemore, Dudley Randall, Hoyt W. Fuller, Margaret Burroughs, Sterling A. Brown, Chancellor Williams, Margaret Walker, James Baldwin, John Henrik Clarke, and others. However, not one of these individuals claimed my attention and memory, forced me to recast my thinking in a number of ways, redefined in a world context what it meant to be a committed Black intellectual, a serious warrior-scholar, a whole and productive person maneuvering on his or her own terms. That role belonged exclusively to the person that I also add to this list—Richard A. Long—a first class thinker-researcher-writer-poet, a philosopher-teacher in love with the profession, and a mentor to all.

I met Dr. Richard A. Long in the early 1970s at Paine College in Augusta, Georgia. I was then Don L. Lee—rough, ragged, hip and tied to Blackness and Africa like Christians to Christmas and grand masters to chess. Upon meeting him, I knew immediately what Hoyt W. Fuller, a dear friend and mentor, meant when he forewarned me by stating, "he is different and unforgettable." How right he was. Richard Long was unafraid of anything, on point about most things, and always ready with a well thought out term, phrase, or idea that would leave me smiling, laughing, and thinking at a more profound level.

This was the Dr. Richard A. Long: small in stature, a yellow-Black African American, long on intellect and explanation, serious as a first love on the absolute necessity of Black culture (art, history, politics, economics, and psychology) to the healthy development of our people, and a dynamite dresser who had no problem changing clothes two or three times a day. He lived his words and work. He could turn a lecture on the significance of Alain Locke's theory on racial relativism into a laugh-fest, interjecting his own personal journey with that of an in-depth history of the time. Arguments so honest, clear, and insightful that one always walked away with a greater appreciation of the subject, the teacher, one's self, and the African/Black world.

One can tell the soul and substance of a person by visiting his or her home. The person's precious living space where he/she spends most of his/her time is critical in defining that person in no uncertain terms. Professor Long's home was exactly what he taught—culturally specific and boldly Black and African. His personal preferences and southern subtlety were quietly and loudly on display. As he walked me through his book-lined, art and music-filled lived-in home, I had no doubts as to who he was and what he wanted us to know about him.

Dr. Long did not have any biological children, yet those of us who were deeply and profoundly changed by his presence all remained his cultural children. It is indeed an honor to be working with close friends Eleanor Traylor and Beverly Guy Sheftall in reintroducing this book of poetry, *Ascending and Other Poems*, which is Dr. Richard A. Long's final gift to us. While Dr. Long is best known for his critical writing and edited collections including the groundbreaking *Afro-American Writing: An Anthology of Prose and Poetry* (co-edited with Eugenia Collier), this superb collection of his own work is a significant part of his continued lifelong cultural work. Our ongoing charge is to learn from him, teach his messages and keep alive his enormous contributions to our culture, our people, and the world. Enough said.

Haki R. Madhubuti
Poet, Founder and Publisher of Third World Press

An Introduction

For those who have come within the sphere of influence of Richard A. Long, there will be no surprise that he writes poetry, nor that his poems are far from conventional. This sometime poet is among those blessed humans about whom there is nothing ordinary. Nor is there strain in his perception of language, nor in the form in which he frames them. The range of experience and concern reflected in these poems is wide and varied, admitting barriers neither of time nor space. They reflect sensitivity, which is open, contoured, and whole.

The broad sweep of images embraces several continents and cultures, personalities of three generations, and revolutions, which are variously real and imagined and still-born. But these images are firmly anchored in the poet's understanding and appreciation of art—of what art is and of what it can never be. The poet's sketches of his times, and of the people, places and ideas which vitalize them, are never sentimental, never cynical, but are etched with candor and tinted with humor.

To read his poems, these articulations of his consciousness and his vision, is to make an imaginative journey with a very special sensibility.

Hoyt W. Fuller
May 5, 1975
Chicago

Ascending
for Beauford

"I don't want to know whom people descend
from. I want to know what they are ascending to."
—Beauford Delaney

It was fall.

The leaves fell, all the colors of the
palette lay on the warm earth, and the
train sped north and east, east and north,
leaving behind Tennessee.

Tennessee and mama and papa and church
and the warm bosoms, the laughter, the sky
and the hills.

Leaving behind the leaves on the warm
earth, all the colors of the palette.

Through the winding tunnels, over mountains
and rivers, north and east, east and
north, the train travelled until Boston.
Boston, land of cold, land of cod, and
gray sky, pearly with chill, and mama and
papa not there. But Boston it was and
the cold cast of Praxiteles to trace
in charcoal on hundreds of sheets of
yellowing paper.

Boston. And Cambridge. And the Fenway.
The high ceilings of the picture-lined rooms.
The muffled voices, the old women in Mrs.
Jack's palace, the music.

For music is the string, the link, the tie.
Rise and fall. Fall and rise. And the
gray sky, pearly with repose, and far
away, Tennessee and the leaves budding
forth from the barren boughs.

So season comes and seasons go. Leaves
bud, and flesh, fall, all the colors of the
palette.

Tennessee. Boston. And so New York.

The tension, the joy. Poets and singers.
The blues and jazz. Opera. For music is
the trace. And the actors and the acted.

And once more the museums, the tall
ceilings, the school of Venice, the school
of Florence, the school of Paris. Once
more the casts of Praxiteles.

And blues and jazz.

And art and music. And music.

The colors, all the colors of the palette.

Green Street. The fine hydrants and the
children. Winter. Summer. High ceilings.

Green Street. Friends. Fires. And
whiteness. The realms of white to catch
the sun.

And green and yellow, the passion of sun
and sky.

And blue and green. Passion of earth, now
distant. In Washington Square, the arch,
arching, arch.

Then, miraculously, the call, the challenge.
The swishing of the sea against the sides
of the ship. Echoes of St. Louis Woman,
Swishing of the sea.

At last the sun of France. The sweep
of Paris. The arc arching. L'Etoile, Les
champs. The Louvre.

The high ceilings, the sweep of history,
color, and form.

Jeu de Paume.

At last the secret of the Orangerie. First,
emanation. First, intuition. First, Discovery.
And at last the secret.

Montparnasse, Clamart, Montparnasse.

The Cycle. The Discovery. The Cycle.

All gathers, comes to growth, fuses.

The yellow, the green. The white paper
catching, refracting the sunlight.

The palette fills with light and love.
The spirit lifts, rises.

The world floats, ascends.

Ascension.

Ascending.

Hearing James Brown at the
Café des Nattes
Sidi Bou Said, Tunisia

Yes, brother, your word has come
                              Don't want nobody
                              Give me nuthin
Crowning this hilltop, long ago's lighthouse
                              Open up the do'
                              Git it myself
Your word comes, thanks God and Macaroni
To this eyrie where I sit
Mint tea before, serenaded by caged birds
And the undulating arias or Arabia,
Her last vestige of empire.

In waves, over the waves it comes
                              Don't want nobody
Mingling with birdsong and arabesques
                              Give me nuthin
Floating over an Andulusian mise-en-scene
(I remember Cordova)
                              Open up the do'
It pierces the blanched housetops, the waiting sea
                              Git it myself

You moan, Dido plunges into the flames
You groan, Hannibal embarks
You shriek, Cato's vow is fulfilled
You sigh, the sea roars beside a silent shore

Flairing into this moment
Your voice, snatched from beyond Sahara's sands
Crosses the western sea, enters familiarly
This concatenation of Africa's time
Flavoring mint, infusing birdsong, merging into the endless
vocalise.

Juan de Pereja
Painted by Velasquez
in memory of Alain Locke

Amused contempt, is it that radiates
    From your velvet domain
Or disgust for the bemused who throng
    The dim ascetic space?

Under the scrutiny of brown eyes and blue
    You view Rome's seven hills
Thinking, perhaps, of vacant yellow sands
    Undulant, limitless.

Though chaotic and obscure the furies
    Who decreed your present part,
Though anguished and confused the hungry eyes
    Feeding upon your flesh,
You mediate the sordid encounter,
    Osculant, putrid, rank,
And regard, serene, the ceaseless discourse
    Of wisdom and folly.

Song

Oh, do not care,
Love, loved, beloved,
If I do not remember you tomorrow,
For tomorrow is a yesterday
And yesterday was blithe and clear
And not unlonely.

Oh, do not care,
Love, loved. beloved,
If we remember
Only parting and sorrow
For today is a tomorrow
And tomorrow is a promise
Whose portion is pain.

Together is as together was,
And may never again
Together be,
Until we are what we were.
So, do not care if care is not,
Oh, love, loved, beloved.

On the Beach

So soft the sun's rays
so soft the breeze
so soft the sea-spray
so soft fingers
on flaring cheeks.

The hard glint of eyes
sullen with rageless pain
subsides, sinks,
soflty accedes
to solemn symbiosis.

Stretched in recall
taut and unrepentant
with no sensation but the ache
on half-remembered regret
you smile
(slowly, carefully, easing the edges of
you lips)
you smile
hollow-cheeked and indifferent
deja vu flooding your mind
parting you lips in farewell.

Verbal
for Mabel Mercer

Each in an eachness much with much
Shapes springful stream to joy and such
Prim primps while quiet mincing words
Severs out from in flight from birds

Late late tiring tires and night falls
To echo of raindrop on walls
Drip pitter drop patter and then
Dreams silly stir now lies by when

Now never know what never why
Firm earth is earth airy sky sky
Never know never know before
Not some and some shut tight the door

A B J

Jazz, joy, jiving
Jig , jog, jungle
Joint, jerk, jabbing
Jaw, jug, jaundice

Juice, junk, jitters
Jot, jet, journey
Joke, jest, jetsam
Jinx, judge, jury

Jam, jar, jelly
June, john, jonquil
Job, jack, jingo
Jim, Joe, Jesus

Phoneme
for Don Lee

Perceive,
it struggles, scrapes
the walls of fleshy overhang
relentless
stricture, counter-stricture
Through the endless vault of purple
past the ivory gates
The softly rounded barrier
o
(silence)

Mid-Winter
Five Haiku

We search depths of glass
milk-hued...a slice of rainbow
melting at the touch.

Lips almost touching
we banter in narrow streets
breathing tracery.

Suddenly cold winds
challenge joy with wordlessness...
lilacs dream of spring.

Words—steel blades clashing.
Regret rejecting regret...
Thorns outlive the rose.

Will birds fly no more
In the empty corridor
Between our closed doors?

Afternoon

Such the silence eternal until noise
Of ten thousand reeds strike the hanging
        air,
Consume the startled hills, crush bees
        who dare
The motion of life in that place, then
        poise
Men for destruction: in the plain burn
        Troys
Innumerable, grander and more fair
Than the ancient town, till, caught
        unaware,
Cataclysm fades in the shouts of boys.

Two stand still in aftermath, stand
        upright,
Eye to eye, fearing to speak lest earth
        quake
Again and release a fresh surge of might.
Silence and eternity, each to slake
The other's speed, press each to each a
        brake,
While pale through haze, through
        gloom falters the night.

Poet Poem

Some say the poet is the lord of language
Some say the poet is the king of words
Some say the poet is time's hostage
I say, a poet ain't nothing but a bird.

He flies/or tries
He chirps/or burbs
He sings/or stings
A poet ain't nothing but a bird

Come the eventide
When the spirit wants to ride
Who's standing by your side?
A poet. Ain't nothin but a bird.

In the mornintime
When your spirit wants to climb
Who can play on your chime?
A poet. Ain't nothing but a bird.

Some like 'em hot/Some like 'em cold
Some like 'em young/Some like 'em old
But a poet ain't nothing but a bird.
And some poets/are chickens.

Blackword: To a Poetess

Don't let's make a stink
Poised out here on the brink
Of Greco-Roman antiquity.

Extend an opalescent hand
Let fall from the brand
Sparkles of sincerity.

Knock out the signifying urge
With ode, epic and dirge
From sea to shining sea.

Dash home before the damp
Light your bedside lamp
And rest in financial security.

Paul Laurence Dunbar
1872 – 1906

Your voice echoes still, warm with poet's desire,
Cool with metre's discipline,
Cracked by love's anxieties.

Your heart, a mirror
Streaked by vain visions
Unworthy of its reflection, bleeds still.

Your fate is a poem,
A lesson for our voices, for our hearts,
Introit to our fate.

Monday

for the Paris Tribe of Hair

Monday is a very funny day
It comes after Sunday
And too soon after Saturday night
Which is a day all by itself.

Monday is mean and evil
It gets into the corners of your eyes
And it makes your head ache
And your mouth taste like bitter pills.

Monday is disagreeable
Like a woman in a kimono
With her hair in paper curlers
And a rolling pin in her hand.

Monday is prejudiced
In favor of white folks
And hates to see a black man
Get even a little bit ahead.

Monday can't dance
And ain't got no rhythm
Clapping its hands on one
And thinking it's some kind of cute.

I don't know what to do about Monday
But I think I'll call a meeting
And bring it up on the carpet
And get its papers taken away.

And then it better not ever
Rear its ugly head again
Scaring all of God's children
Looking like a hurrah's nest.

Grass Widow

He's a liquor head
And what's more he dips snuff.
Mama always said
His best wouldn't be enough.

It was yesterday
Around about five o'clock
Child came in from play
When I heard him down the block.

Coming home again
Like he always used to do
With some of the men
Cooked in the same pot of stew.

I greeted him nice.
Welcomed him back from the dead.
Now he's pressing ice
On top of his nappy head.

Niggers is People
for Hoyt Fuller

If you coming to town
STAND UP STRAIGHT, and don't clown.
Watch it! Tuck in them lips.
And stop swinging them hips.
Folks may not know your name:
They watching just the same.

It makes me mad to hear
Heeing and hawing clear
Across the street and back
Like some train off the track.
In the street, what the heck
You s'posed to act correct.

Not a word, not a sound
Else you gon be put down
Don't smack gum, don't break wind
And if you ain't yet been,
Go!
Niggers is people.

Godfather

A few...hours [spent with one another]
can affect the outcome of whole lifetimes.
—Arundhati Roy

It was David Dorsey, a leading scholar on African Literature, who introduced me to the Center for African and African American Studies in the late sixties. David Dorsey was representative of an age of genius and a conduit for the legendary force of Richard A. Long. At Atlanta University, Dr. Long was among such distinguished faculty as Clarence Bacote, Robert Brisbane, Hubert and Edyth Ross, Richard Barksdale, Thomas Jarret, and Lucy Grigsby. Dr. Long, founder of the Center for African and African American Studies, was defining knowledge in the Academy. His involvement in the Afro American Movement contributed to the rise of a new cultural critique deeply rooted in and reflective of Black literature and folklore. His critical voice, that guiding hand laid on me the day I met Dr. Long remains life changing and life enhancing.

Godfather is the name that reflects Dr. Long's historical, legendary, and mythical life. I cannot be sure, but it was likely my mother who first gave him the name. Through nose-and-palate memory, I still savor the turnip-green-cornbread-roast chicken offering at one of Richard's "gatherings" at my mother's house. Through the imperfect eye of memory I see the biblical beauty of Hoyt W. Fuller, founding editor of *Negro Digest* to become *Black World* and to evolve as *First World Magazine*; Toni Cade Bambara, who would become a major novelist; Earl Clowney, professor of Francophone literature; and Sam Floyd – through whom I met, in his book-lined Greenwich Village apartment, Verta Mae Grosvenor, Paule Marshall, Nina Simone, Dolly McPherson, and Maya Angelou. Jerry Ward and Eugenia Collier—professor-artist-activists—may have been there, but I recall David sitting next to me in my mother's home. He smiled when my mother turned to Dr. Long and called him Godfather.

Dr. Long was a reference point, a geo-political educator. He brought his Fellows of the Conference on African and African

American Studies to the living rooms of sung and unsung storytellers, including Miss Lou (Louise Bennett), Rex Nettleford (to become the Honourable), and Mr. Coverley of Jamaica; curator Pierre Monosiet in Haiti; Dr. Abdias do Nascimento in Brazil; poet Robin Dobre, since martyred, in Surinam; Romare and Nannette Bearden in St. Martin; Gordon Heath, Lee Payant, and Benny Luke (later Bob Tomlinson) in Paris; Louise Meriwether, Rosa Guy, and Joan Sandler in New York. This list is not comprehensive, but intended to underscore the vitality of Dr. Long's Legacy.

That moment when Afro-America assesses its intellectual capital, it can rejoice in an inexhaustible banquet. The historical moment that Dr. Long so graciously invited young people into was a moment that grounded his 1993 text *African Americans: A Portrait*. This book, along with others of its era, erases what Chester Everett observed as "a lingering impression...that Afro American (Black) writing and Black (consciousness) has an immaculate conception and a virgin birth one troubled night in the late sixties and in an insurgent alley in Watts..." Dr. Long nurtured those who would give strength and breadth to the cultural arm of the pervasive Movement. He is, to borrow his own language, "fiber-deep in the warp and woof of Afro-American life," he is, as he wrote of Dr. Du Bois, James Weldon Johnson, and Alain Leroy Locke, "pioneer mentor" of generations. Of mine, he remains Godfather.

Eleanor W. Traylor
Sterling Brown Professor and Graduate Professor of
English at Howard University

About the Author

Richard A. Long received both the A.B. and the M.A. degree from Temple University in 1947 and 1948 respectively. In 1948 and 1949, he studied at the University of Pennsylvania. The summer of 1950 was spent at Oxford and that of 1954 in Paris. From 1958 to 1959, Mr. Long was a Fulbright Scholar at the University of Paris. In 1965, he received the Doctorate (D. es L.) from the University of Poitiers.

His professional experience has been richly varied. Mr. Long has taught at Atlanta University and the University of Poitiers. Between **1956 and 1971, Mr. Long, talented as an entrepreneur, conducted** several special projects including seminars, symposiums, exhibits and conferences on Haitian Art and Culture, Primitive Art, African Art, African-American Studies, etc.

The poet has had numerous professional affiliations, including being a professional affiliations, including being President of the College Language Association; President of the Southeastern Conference of Linguistics; Member of Manpower Committee, Linguistic Society of America. He serves on the Editorial Board of *Phylon*, **Papers in** *Linguistics* **and** *Black Books Bulletin*. **Mr. Long is** currently Director of the Center for African and African-American Studies at Atlanta University. Though he has had numerous articles in so many learned publications, this, his first volume of poetry, reveals yet another facet of the creativity of a brilliant **scholar of the highest rank.**

Margaret T. Burroughs
(1975)

Richard Long—a celebrated author, lecturer, cultural historian, and the Atticus Haygood Professor of Interdisciplinary Studies, Emeritus, at Emory University—began his career in academia teaching English at West Virginia State College and Morgan State College. While completing his doctoral work, he also worked as a lecturer at the University of Poitiers. Upon returning to the United States, he taught English and French for the Hampton Institute and directed its College Museum. In addition, he has worked as a visiting lecturer to universities in West, Central and South Africa, and India.

He founded the Triennial Symposium on African Art, Atlanta University's Annual Conference at the Center for African and African American Studies, and the New World Festivals of the African Diaspora. He was a U.S. committee member at the Second World Black and African Festival of Arts and Culture in Lagos, Nigeria, from 1971 to 1977 and has acted as a consultant for both the National Endowment for the Arts and the National Endowment for the Humanities.

He lectured widely on a variety of topics and has served as a consultant to many cultural organizations and institutions.

(2013)